Architecture of the Absurd

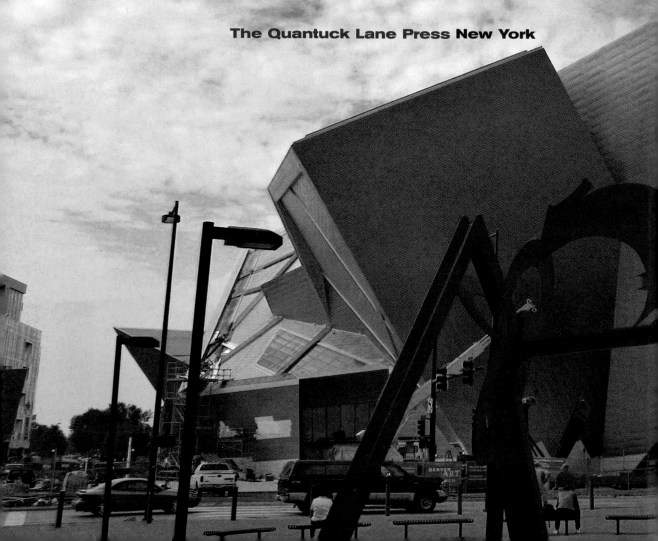

Architecture

How "Genius" Disfigured a Practical Art

John Silber

The Quantuck Lane Press New York

of the Absurd

Architecture of the Absurd

How "Genius" Disfigured a Practical Art

Copyright © 2007 by John Silber
Since this page cannot legibly accommodate all the permissions and copyright notices, page 94 constitutes an extension of the copyright page.

Manufacturing by Mondadori Printing, Verona

Library of Congress Cataloging-in-Publication Data

Silber, John.
   Architecture of the absurd : how "genius" disfigured a practical art /
John Silber. — 1st ed.
      p. cm.
   ISBN 978-1-59372-027-8
  1. Architecture—Human factors. 2. Creation (Literary, artistic, etc.)
3. Absurd (Philosophy) in art. 4. Architects and patrons. 5. Architecture and society.
I. Title.
NA2542.4.S53 2007
724'.6--dc22

                                        2007029651

The Quantuck Lane Press
New York
www.quantucklanepress.com

Distributed by: W.W. Norton & Company, 500 Fifth Avenue, New York, NY 10110
www.wwnorton.com
W.W. Norton & Company Ltd., Castle House, 75/76 Wells Street, London, WIT 3QT

1 2 3 4 5 6 7 8 9 0

In memory of my father,

Paul George Silber, AIA

1881–1957

Contents

Acknowledgments

I wish to express my thanks to Dr. Chandler Rosenberger, who has served as my research assistant and, among other contributions, has collected all of the illustrations I requested, many of which he has traveled far and wide to photograph himself. In addition, he has been a careful reader and editor whose opinions on this subject have been illuminating. I also wish to thank my executive assistant, Ms. Kelly O'Connor, whose learning, intellectual independence, and sharp eyes have made her an invaluable editor. I am also grateful to James Mairs, who brought to this project the enthusiasm, discernment, and taste for which he is rightly renowned, and to his able assistant, Austin O'Driscoll.

Finally, I must express my gratitude to my father, Paul George Silber, who engaged me even as a child in the study and practice of architecture and instilled in me a lifelong interest and love for the subject. I dedicate this book to his memory.

Introduction

As a professor of philosophy and law and as a former president of
Boston University, I may seem an unlikely person to write a book on
architecture. But it is not really surprising for three reasons: first, my
education in architecture by working with my father; second, my habit
of studying buildings wherever I have been in the course of travel
that has taken me to many cities, towns, and villages, not only in the
Americas and Europe but also in the Middle East and Asia; and third,
my extensive involvement over thirty years in the planning and construction of buildings at Boston University.

My father was an architect trained in Berlin in the Beaux-Arts tradition, a school of design dedicated to architecture that is both beautiful
and practical. The curriculum he studied included design, engineering,
and sculpture. He came to the United States in 1902 as a sculptor to assist in the construction of the German Pavilion at the St. Louis World's
Fair of 1904. Fascinated by this country of "one thousand possibilities,"
he remained here, and after some travel and various employments he
began his architectural practice in Palestine, Texas. His practice flourished and soon he moved to San Antonio, where many more opportuni-
ties were offered. In the second and third decades of the twentieth century he was fully occupied with the design and construction of banks,
churches, schools, hotels, and residences. But he was totally lacking in
the political skills and political connections by which to win commissions for public buildings, and his practice withered following the onset
of the Great Depression. From 1931 to 1941, his practice was limited to
an occasional new residence or small building and more frequently to
projects calling only for renovation or remodeling of existing structures.

During the war he designed and supervised construction of military bases including large assembly and mess halls. With steel reserved for war production, his Beaux-Arts knowledge of wooden trusses and arches served the war effort. After the war his civilian practice flourished again.

From the time I was eight until I was twenty-three, my father called on me from time to time to assist him. He used me most often in that bleak pre-war period when I helped him measure buildings he had been engaged to remodel. Along the way I learned to read blueprints and specifications and I could relate elevations and cross sections to floor plans without difficulty. My father also talked to me extensively about the history of architecture and the expectations and requirements imposed on the responsible architect. Without recourse to books, he would discuss works of architects and sculptors he admired, works by Praxiteles, Brunelleschi, Michelangelo, Palladio, Wright's great mentor Louis Sullivan, and such modern architects as Richard Neutra and Eero Saarinen.

I frequently had the opportunity to observe my father on the job. He explained that two percent of his fee was to inspect all stages of construction to ensure that the client's interests were fully met by the exact execution of plans and specifications. He would personally supervise jobs such as pouring concrete or setting plumbing, where no evidence of sloppiness or omission would be visible once they were finished, but he also visited the construction site after five p.m. when the contractor and workmen were gone. He would examine everything in detail and take notes for a meeting the following morning with the contractor. If he had specified that all the surfaces of the doors were to be sealed, he would hold a small mirror above the top of the door and below its bottom edge to see that these surfaces, not directly observable once the doors were hung, had been painted or varnished. And if he had specified three coats of paint—a primer and two finish coats—he would wait until the first finish coat was done and then come in after five p.m. to make little pencil marks at different locations. After the contractor reported that the final coat was done, my father would return to check his pencil marks. If any had not been covered by the final finish coat, my father called the contractor to task and saw that the work was done as specified. Contractors soon learned that there were no shortcuts on my father's jobs, and clients knew they could rely on him.

My father sharpened my skills in the summer of 1949 when he hired me briefly as a draftsman in his office. He gave me a floor plan and elevation and asked me to draw a cross section at a line designated. In drafting a cross section I had to produce an elevation, drawn to scale, of what one would see from the perspective of the section indicated on the floor plan. After drafting a cross section, I was assigned the design of a staircase where the ratio of risers to treads was two to three. I had to determine the height of the risers, the width of treads, and the number of steps required to climb comfortably from the lower to the upper floor. Once the assignment was completed, my father checked carefully, including all calculations. He expected no errors and with his help I learned to meet that standard.

This experience made me more observant—appreciative or critical—of every building I saw. On a trip to Europe in 1971, my son and I looked at many buildings in England, Scotland, Germany, and Italy. We took scores of photographs of the good, the bad, and the ugly. The last group, we decided, would make an amusing illustrated book—*Original Sin in Architecture*. We were also inspired by the magnificent creations of Christopher Wren, the medieval cathedrals whose designers and creators were unknown, and the palaces, churches, and grand houses of Venice, Florence, and Rome.

Although my knowledge of the history of architecture and my experience in studying buildings and drafting were useful when I taught classes in aesthetics, it never occurred to me that all I had learned from my father would be put to constant use as a university president. Oversight of Boston University's building program, including new construction, renovation and remodeling of existing buildings and the selection of architects and contractors, was an important part of my responsibilities. Our building program over a quarter of a century totaled 13,729,143 square feet. It included classroom buildings, science and research buildings, a school of management topped by an administrative center, several dormitories, a bookstore, convenience centers, a boathouse, a field house, a fitness center, and a 6,500-seat arena. It also included the construction of major medical facilities and the renovation and preservation of thirty-three elegant town houses for dormitories and academic centers. In overseeing these projects my prior experience proved invaluable.

Some architects were initially bothered by my ability to read plans and specifications, and were occasionally put off when I dismissed their elaborate, high-flown aesthetic justifications of design features as gratuitous bloviation. On one occasion when I noticed that the plan showed a chase intersecting a supporting beam, I asked the architect how he would support the severed beam. I understood his embarrassment and assured him that such rare mistakes were bound to occur in the preparation of a complex set of drawings. From that time on we worked well together in the completion of several buildings.

Knowing Boston University's financial limits, I insisted on designs that did not require unnecessarily complex and costly construction. When for example a grand atrium was designed to be carried from the ground floor to the top of a nine-story building, I insisted instead that it terminate in an apparent skylight at the ceiling level of the sixth floor. The atrium on the first six floors, surrounded by classrooms and faculty offices, was designed to facilitate communication among faculty and students of the School of Management. But there were no such needs on the seventh, eighth, and ninth floors, which were devoted to administrative offices and functions. By eliminating the atrium on the top three floors we added about 40 percent additional space at a substantially reduced cost.

For all of these projects I selected architects and contractors who were responsive to our needs. As this book makes clear, I have never been impressed by architects who think they are fine artists first and builders only second. Instead I looked for firms whose principals found their creative satisfaction in meeting a wide range of their clients' practical needs while also adding handsome buildings to Boston's landscape. Fortunately the university found brilliant and practical architects in such firms as Cannon Design, The Architects Collaborative, the Stubbins Associates, and Architectural Resources, and skilled craftsmen and supervisors in the construction firm Walsh Brothers, Inc.

My involvement in the design and construction of so many buildings led to my being nominated as an honorary member of the American Institute of Architects. On May 11, 2002, I was elected and proudly became a member of the organization to which my father had belonged for so many years.

As a consequence of my election to the AIA, I was invited by the Texas Society of Architects to address its convention in Fort Worth, Texas, on October 31, 2003. In addressing that crowd of four thousand architects, I took as my topic "Architecture of the Absurd." The book that follows is an expansion of that address.

Architecture of the Absurd

I

In 1951 the internationally renowned architect Harwell Hamilton Harris was appointed director of the School of Architecture at the University of Texas. Along with his dynamic wife, Jean, he recruited a group of brilliant young artists and architects to the school's faculty. This group of Young Turks—Bernard Hoesli, Colin Rowe, Robert Slutzky, John Hejduk, Lee Hirsche, and Lee Hodgden—gathered regularly in the late afternoons or evenings to discuss aspects of art, architecture, aesthetics, and Gestalt psychology. I joined the faculty of the University of Texas shortly after their recruitment, and Bob Slutzky, who knew me and my interest in aesthetics and architecture from our association at Yale, invited me to participate in their informal seminars.

These intense young men were determined to develop a new and superior curriculum for the education of aspiring architects. Colin Rowe and Robert Slutzky were the principal and most articulate theorists of the group; together they wrote *Transparency*. After circulating underground for forty years it was finally published in 1997 and became required reading in architecture schools. The book defined a program of architecture that, recognizing the limitations of both the Beaux-Arts and Bauhaus programs, sought to find a reconciliation of what was valid in each while avoiding their arbitrary restrictions. It also attempted to find a common ground of understanding in the seemingly diverse views of Frank Lloyd Wright and Le Corbusier and to consider the implications of Gestalt psychology for architectural design.[1]

Rowe and Slutzky's basic idea, that an architect's understanding and use of space can be enhanced by the knowledge of how space is read and understood by painters, was developed in the vigorous give and take of those early discussions. It was at these sessions that Rowe and Slutzky developed their novel ideas on transparency which were to become so influential. They contrasted the literal, obvious transparency of the Bauhaus and the Barcelona Pavilion with the phenomenal transparency in the facades and interiors of Renaissance buildings and, surprisingly, in the innocent frontier architecture of Lockhart, Texas.

1 Walter Gropius. Bauhaus, Dessau (1925–26).

2 Ludwig Mies van der Rohe. German Pavilion, International Art Exhibition (1928-9; rebuilt, 1959).
Erich Lessing / Art Resource, NY.
© 2007 Artists Rights Society (ARS), New York/VG Bild-Kunst, Bonn.

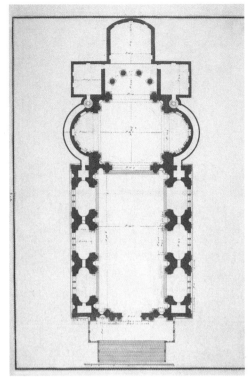

3 Andrea Palladio. Church of the Redentore, Venice (1576). Toward the apse.
Cameraphoto Arte, Venice/
Art Resource, NY.

4 Palladio. Church of the Redentore. Plan.
Archivision Inc.

5 Henry E. M. Guidon. Caldwell County Courthouse, Lockhart, TX. (1894).
© 2004 John Siebel Photography.

6 San Marco, Venice (1076).
Cameraphoto/Art Resource.

To illustrate their ideas, they offered several examples of phenomenal transparency, including the transparent wall defined by four columns separating the apse from the nave in the Church of the Redentore and the transparent wall dividing the space of the Square of San Marco in Venice. Three tall, precisely aligned flagpoles create a transparent wall dividing the smaller space between the poles and the church from the larger space of the rest of the square. Rowe and Slutzky had developed a new way to think about architectural space. Their conception of transparencies and the advocacy of their use in architectural design, however, was not an endorsement of the literal transparencies of the International Style, as the Bauhaus program was known after Gropius and Mies van der Rohe immigrated to the United States.

After participating in several sessions, I was asked to speak and took as my topic why there would never be an architecture of the absurd. I recognized that remarkably silly houses or buildings might occasionally be built, but I argued that corporate, educational, philanthropic, governmental, and medical institutions and individual persons of wealth would never support an architectural movement in which lead-ing architects would attempt to advance their careers by the design of major structures that were absurd, structures that failed to meet the needs—functional, aesthetic, and economic—of the client.

"Absurd" is not difficult to define. The Oxford English Dictionary defines absurd as "inharmonious, tasteless, foolish"; in music "jarring and out of tune"; and more broadly "out of harmony with reason or propriety, incongruous, unreasonable, illogical." The OED cites a particularly relevant quotation in which the absurd is illustrated by "caprice... in preferring absurdity of invention to correct imitation."

Architecture, I argued, would never develop along the lines of the theater of the absurd, which peaked at about the time I was speaking with celebrations of works by Albert Camus and especially Samuel Beckett's *Waiting for Godot*. I insisted that architecture would not follow the course of art as exemplified by Robert Rauschenberg's series of *White Paintings* or the course of music that captured the essence of the absurd in John Cage's 1952 composition *4'33"* (four minutes and thirty-three seconds of silence). Painters, sculptors, and composers were being rewarded by foundations and academic institutions for engaging in the "absurdity of invention." And often they were celebrated for mere boldness in the absence of purposeful innovation.

In music, for example, the Fromm Foundation supported minimalism, serialism, and any other trend in music that abjured melody, harmony, and tonality; it favored those musicians who showed contempt for any music that might attract a large public and provide livelihood for the composer.

Instead, the foundation and other patrons of the arts sponsored academic poets, painters, and composers who, for the most part, made their livings in colleges or universities and created not to please a large and receptive audience, but rather to please their colleagues and elitist peers. Commissions went to composers whose new works would likely receive their one and only performance financed by the sponsor. Artists, but especially musicians and poets, typically disdained Dr. Samuel Johnson's view that "no man but a blockhead ever wrote except for money." Rather, in the last half of the twentieth century artists increasingly earned their livings not by their art but by teaching. There was critical contempt for artists who made their livings as artists while also creating works that illuminate the human condition. (Shakespeare, Michelangelo, Beethoven, Rembrandt, Van Dyck, Goethe, Wagner, Verdi, and Puccini, of course, had no such scruples.)

However, in architecture, I argued, the architect's relationships to his client and to the intended occupants of his building define the boundaries of his profession. This is in part what distinguishes an architect from a sculptor. The aesthetics of a building, in contrast to the aesthetics of a piece of sculpture, are judged according to how well a building fulfills a client's goals and the requirements of those who live and work within it. No one lives and works in a sculpture; unlike a work of architecture, it is an aesthetic object and is observed from without.

The architect must know how to meet the requirements of his profession efficiently. He must understand the art of the possible as it applies to the construction of buildings, and he must know the relative merits of various means of achieving his ends. The architect may leverage his own knowledge and abilities by the use of engineers and estimators. But he still needs to know enough to assess the reasonableness of their recommendations, for he is ultimately responsible for the completed work.

In the discussion that followed my talk, Colin Rowe asked: Weren't the follies constructed in the eighteenth and nineteenth centuries in England examples of absurd architecture? I replied that these structures were an expression of romanticism, nostalgia for a classical past. Although they were artificial, they were harmonious structures that lent a sense of antiquity and coherence to the grounds of large estates.

Bob Slutzky then asked my opinion of the work of Antonio Gaudí: Couldn't one make a case for the absurdity of the roof vents and chimneys and even the facade of the Casa Milà, or the facade and dragon roof of the Casa Batlló?

I insisted that these structures, including the specific features mentioned by Slutzky, are all functional, harmonious, and offer no offense to their neighbors.

7 David Ferrand. St. David's Ruin. Harden Grange, England (1976).

8 Antonio Gaudí. Casa Milà,
Barcelona (1906–10), roof.

9 Gaudí. Casa Batlló, Barcelona
(1904–06), roof detail.

Consider the aerial view of the Casa Milà showing its roof and those of its neighbors. Is it not more interesting and harmonious than the clutter of the neighboring roofs?

Güell Park, with its serpentine benches and giant sculptured animals, is delightfully functional.

10 Gaudí. Güell Park, Barcelona (1884–87).

11 Gaudí. Güell Park, Barcelona (1884-87).
Vanni/Art Resource.

12 Gaudí. Sagrada Familia, Barcelona (1883-present).

Vanni/Art Resource.

Antonio Gaudí was a devout Catholic and would have regarded the intrusion of any absurdity in the Sagrada Familia as sacrilege. His cathedral is, rather, the expression of his religious passion.

Gaudí's integration of sculpted figures into Sagrada Familia's facade is different from the integration of sculptures into the entrances of Gothic cathedrals, but neither is absurd.

The canting of supporting columns was not absurd but the result of creative engineering that met the load demands of the building's structure.

13 Gaudí. Sagrada Familia, exterior detail.

14 Notre Dame, Paris (1160-1350). Tympanum on west facade.
Timothy McCarthy/Art Resource.

15 Gaudí. Sagrada Familia,
passion facade.

16 Gaudí. Sagrada Familia,
wire model.

Gaudí determined the angles of his columns according to the strict requirements of his design. He made a wire model of the building with articulated segments that, when turned upside down, allowed gravity to demonstrate the angles at which the columns should lean. He then built a solid model along the lines revealed.

Far from irrational or absurd, the Sagrada Familia revealed Gaudí's genius in finding new ways to achieve his vision—always surprising but also functional, harmonious, inspiring, and beautiful.

I find it illuminating to compare Gaudí's Sagrada Familia with Simon Rodia's Watts Towers.

Rodia was a primitive, the Grandma Moses of architecture—a folk genius. All the instincts of a weaverbird were expressed in the construction of his monumental towers built without a plan, except as it was implicit in his consciousness. With scrap metal and wire and with porcelain shards implanted decoratively in cement, in the manner of Gaudí, Rodia built so well that his one-hundred-foot towers, when tested, withstood winds of two hundred miles per hour. There is no trace of absurdity but dignity, aspiration, and triumph in Rodia's towers.

In insisting to my young colleagues that there would never be an architecture of the absurd, I took for granted that no client of sound mind would pay for the design and construction of an absurdity. I also believed that no architect would consider an absurd building as the fulfillment of his professional responsibilities.

But after seeing what has happened to architecture in the past few decades, all I can say is: How could I have been so wrong?

17 Simon Rodia. Watts Towers, Los Angeles, CA (1921–57).

18 Rodia. Watts Towers, detail.

II

I thought I was on solid ground in 1956 in denying the possibility of an absurd movement in architecture. My faith in my theory continued for the next few years but was gradually eroded as I witnessed the increasing domination of absurdism in other artistic fields and its eventual spread to architecture.

The absurdity movement spread as a cadre of self-proclaimed artists—painters, sculptors, performance artists—arose who would do anything to attract large audiences. These artists rejected the security of the academy and sought celebrity by any means.

Professor Donald Weismann, who in the 1950s was chairman of the Art Department at the University of Texas, Austin, and a decade later a member of the council of the National Endowment for the Arts, lectured on art for years to classes of four hundred students. Forty years ago, in 1967, he told his students:

> **We got to a point in the social history of contemporary art where NOVELTY—far out, outrageous difference with whatever is current at the time—appears as the raison d'être for an artist's notoriety called "success." If the painting, or whatever, is not SOMETHING NEW, something shocking, outlandish, tabooed, generally unprecedented, it doesn't attract the attention of the public in large numbers and thereby not the dealers' interest.[2]**

His assessment of the art scene prompted him ten years later to publish *The 12 Cadavers of Joe Mariner*,[3] a novel about an artist who collected twelve embalmed human corpses "to display in New York as [his] first one-man show." In the prologue to the second edition of the novel, Weismann described the corpses: "they'd all be naked, real and standing in various positions and places in a regular high class art gallery." Writing in 2002, Weismann added, "I presume that doesn't sound very far out now, but I was saying this 34 years ago, long before a 53-year-old refugee from the former East Germany who goes by the name von Hagens opened an exhibition in Mannheim, Germany... at that city's Museum of Technology and Work." Those who keep up with these latest developments know that von Hagens's exhibition, which travels to various countries, involves human figures, actual cadavers preserved in plastic, severely carved up to reveal bones, muscles, and tendons.

Gunther von Hagens's notoriety has inspired imitators. In 2005 Premier Exhibitions, a firm that had earned more than $6 million dis-

19 Promotional pamphlet for
Gunther von Hagens's
"Korperwelten" (1999).

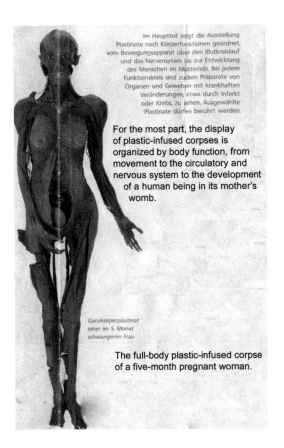

Im Hauptteil zeigt die Ausstellung
Plastinate nach Körperfunktionen geordnet,
vom Bewegungsapparat über den Blutkreislauf
und das Nervensytem bis zur Entwicklung
des Menschen im Mutterleib. Bei jedem
Funktionskreis sind zudem Präparate von
Organen und Geweben mit krankhaften
Veränderungen, etwa durch Infarkt
oder Krebs, zu sehen. Ausgewählte
Plastinate dürfen berührt werden.

For the most part, the display
of plastic-infused corpses is
organized by body function, from
movement to the circulatory and
nervous system to the development
of a human being in its mother's
womb.

Ganzkörperplastinat
einer im 5. Monat
schwangeren Frau

The full-body plastic-infused corpse
of a five-month pregnant woman.

playing artifacts from the *Titanic*, made the logical move from disturbing gravesites to desecrating corpses. In its show "Bodies…the Exhibition," Premier Exhibitions displayed twenty-two full corpses in various states of dissection. Some were hollowed out until nothing but bone, tendons, and nerves remained; others were preserved entirely but sliced into segments, like pieces of sausage.

The corpses in both shows are presented in roughly the way proposed by Weismann in his novel: "in positions of doing ordinary things so that visitors to the exhibition must be constrained—kept from trying to shake hands or dance with those corpses," which, Weismann suggests, "give off the general effects of having been taken from an incinerator after losing all their skin and parts of their anatomy." Weismann makes the point that "von Hagens appears to enjoy and encourages people to think of those brutalized corpses as his works of art."

Joe Mariner, by contrast, eventually recognizes the outrage of his own exhibition—its violation of the sanctity of human beings. He closes the exhibition, removes the corpses, and takes them reverently to ground in places appropriate to each. I find no such redeeming insight in von Hagens or those who view his exhibition with approbation.[4]

Von Hagens's work exemplifies an aesthetic of outrage now common in all fields of art. As Herbert Muschamp, former chief architecture critic of the *New York Times*, proclaimed, "The ideal of 'not pleasing' is fundamental to modern art and modern criticism." Celebrating the "aristocratic satisfaction" of ignoring ordinary people's tastes, Muschamp argued in favor of designs that stand a chance of "kicking up a storm." "The fight itself," he claimed, "is worth fighting for."[5] John Rockwell, the *Times*'s chief art critic, recently celebrated an award-winning work of art that featured "inflatable sex toys performing unprintable acts" and a sculpture of a "decomposed human corpse and other animal parts hanging from a tree." The work, Rockwell admitted, was "truly disturbing" but, he asserted, "great art is always shocking."[6]

Edward Albee, a playwright accomplished in the arts of the absurd, has recently gotten into the act of defending the aesthetics of outrage. Teaching a master class at Emerson College, Albee told students that "each play is an act of aggression against the status quo. Too many playwrights let the audience off the hook instead of slugging them in the face, which is what you should be doing."[7]

Muschamp, Rockwell, and Albee reflect a consensus in the world of contemporary art, theater, and now architecture: art that shocks is the only art that will endure. But as the novelist Tom Wolfe has written, "If Michelangelo's *David, Bacchus,* or *Moses* was regarded as shocking, it has escaped my historical eye."[8] Wolfe need not have limited his observation to Michelangelo. Few have read the *Iliad* and the *Odyssey,* Pindar's elegies, the plays of Sophocles, or the works of Eliot and Austen for the frisson of outrage.

The causes or origins of the view espoused by those who believe that "all great art is shocking" are not aesthetic, but they are readily apparent. First and foremost, burgeoning wealth and consequent materialism support an instant culture of insatiability, which in turn demands novelty—novelty gone stale after "fifteen minutes of fame."[9] The drive toward absurdism in art has accompanied a decline in standards of taste in popular music and movies and the prevalence of tattoos and body-piercing ornamentation; it has been sped by the undeniable influence on architects of painters and sculptors from avant-garde movements and collectives such as Earth Art and Ant Farm.

Each artist offers an elaborate explanation describing some connection between the work of art and a favorite ideology—the protection of the environment or the baleful omnipresence of materialism, etc.

Among the Earth artists, Robert Smithson was remarkably successful in finding patrons to finance his gigantic works. His magnificent *Spiral Jetty* on the Great Salt Lake, Utah, is perhaps the finest work by an artist in this movement. He knew that visitors who walk the coil inward toward its center and then follow its spiral back out will experience first the imprisonment of the human spirit and then, on the return, its liberating expansion. Nothing absurd in this work of art.[10]

Smithson's design for a "Floating Island" is another matter. On his death Smithson left a very crude sketch that shows a large barge filled with dirt, planted with trees, and towed by a tug around New York.

20 Robert Smithson. *Floating Island,* New York, NY (1970). Drawing.
James Cohan Gallery. Art © Estate of Robert Smithson/Licensed by VAGA, New York, NY.

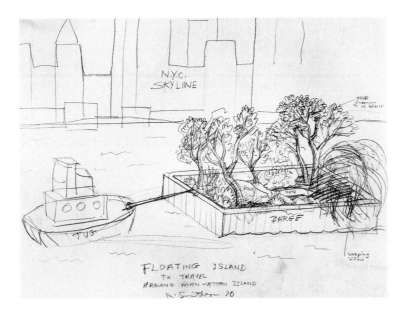

21 Smithson. *Floating Island,* New York, NY (2005).
Robert Caplin/The New York Times/ Redux.

Whatever Smithson may have thought of this project, he did nothing to complete it.

But Smithson may have inspired its completion by succumbing to Theoryspeak, to borrow Tom Wolfe's apt term. In a different context Smithson mused that "the wasted remains of ontology, cosmology, and epistemology still offer a ground for art" at a time when "museums and parks are graveyards above ground—congealed memories of the past that act as a pretext for reality."[11] These words may have inspired the Whitney Museum when in September 2005 it seized on such theorizing to resurrect *Floating Island*. The Whitney justified its decision in luxurious Theoryspeak by describing *Floating Island* as "an homage to Frederick Law Olmsted's design of Central Park," one that "offers a displacement of the park—itself a man-made creation—from its natural habitat."[12]

Floating Island, in fact, does nothing of the sort. Olmsted devoted himself to the preservation and enhancement of the natural habitat of Central Park, leaving in place its huge boulders and hills and dales so that it would not appear to be a man-made Disneyland. The barge pulled around Manhattan did not honor Olmsted or resemble the park. It looked rather like trees and shrubs en route to landscape a billionaire's home in the Hamptons. The Whitney, abandoning thought to wallow in theory, reduced Smithson's sketch to a moving absurdity.

This project of the Whitney Museum confirms my belief that a work of art should be self-contained and its meaning apparent without

22 Doug Michels. *Cadillac Ranch,* **Amarillo, TX (1974).**

extensive verbalization, if only to avoid misunderstandings once text and art part company. In future years, some art historian will doubtless write a scholarly treatise on Doug Michels's *Cadillac Ranch* as an allusion to the Moai figures of Easter Island.

In architecture, the absurd sometimes intrudes by accident into an otherwise beautiful building. In designing the headquarters of the John Hancock Mutual Life Insurance Company,[13] I. M. Pei—with the assistance of engineers and after exhaustive planning—constructed a beautiful tower designed to be a mosaic of its surroundings as they were mirrored in its surface. Unfortunately, the dynamics of the building were such that the six- by twelve-foot panes of glass cracked and fell to the ground with such frequency that it was soon known as the largest plywood building in the world.

The results were absurd. The absurdity was not intentional, however, for if it could have been executed as intended it would have met the needs and expectations of its clients. Rather, the absurdity resulted from a combination of mistakes, some material and some conceptual. Gerhard Bleicken, the CEO of Hancock, asked Arthur Metcalf, a distinguished scientist and engineer and the CEO of Electronics Corporation of America, to attend a meeting on this problem and to advise on solutions. In attempting to justify his design, Pei said that his windows were designed to withstand the one-hundred-year wind. Metcalf instantly identified Pei's key conceptual errors. The hundred-year wind, Metcalf pointed out, is only a statistical concept. It might not take one hundred

23 Moai Figures, Easter Island.
Jorge Provenza/Art Resource, NY.

24 I. M. Pei. John Hancock
Tower, Boston, MA (1973),
under repair.

25 Pei. John Hancock Tower, repaired.

years; it might blow tomorrow and for the next ten days. And, he added, there are no *windows* in the Hancock Tower because Pei had decided to make the *walls* out of glass. Medieval cathedrals, Metcalf observed, have huge wall segments made of glass. But the glass walls do not break in high winds because each pane of glass is small and all flex in their lead cames.

To solve the problem, Metcalf suggested replacing each six- by twelve-foot pane with three panes four by six. The mullions would not block the view of most adults, whose average eye level is higher than four feet and lower than eight. He also noted that the mosaic would be embellished by reducing the size of each tessera. Instead of implementing Metcalf's simple and inexpensive solution, which would have enhanced the beauty of the building, the Hancock company followed Pei's decision and spent millions of dollars to replace all panes with new and heavier glass designed to set off an alarm before shattering in order to permit timely removal.

Although for the most part the failures were in materials and engineering, Pei, as principal architect, was responsible. Pei was also responsible for choosing a foundation engineer for the project whose practice was primarily in New York. This New Yorker, accustomed to laying foundations on solid granite, had scant experience with foundations constructed on piles sunk into landfill over a body of water. Pei passed over Leo Casagrande, a Harvard professor of soil mechanics and an expert on building foundations on the filled land of Boston's Back Bay. Casagrande, who designed and supervised the foundations of the Prudential Tower in 1964, avoided damaging the water table of the Back Bay by using hydraulic pressure to sink coffer dams and piles. Pile drivers were used in constructing the Hancock Tower, however, and their jarring impulses disrupted the water table. Hancock had to spend additional millions to settle legal claims brought by Trinity Church and the Park Plaza Hotel, which were damaged when the water table sank and their piles began to rot.

Correcting the tower's flaws eventually cost the Hancock company $34 million, or about one quarter of the building's original price. A design is genuinely absurd when it is so flawed that it costs millions to correct, and then only partially, for panes continue to shatter and must be constantly monitored. The Hancock Tower illuminates absurdity in architectural practice. Still, it is not an example of the architecture of the absurd for it is now a stunningly beautiful and efficient building.

But what can one say with regard to the intrusion of a glass pyramid into the courtyard of the Louvre?

One must acknowledge the marked improvement Pei made by relocating the entrance to the Louvre underground through the pyramid. But why didn't he locate the pyramid and the entrance two hundred feet to the west so that the view of the seventeenth-century courtyard is not spoiled by the inharmonious and intrusive presence of a late-twentieth-century structure? Was he prevented by city officials? If not, he is responsible for creating a constant disturbing tension between the pyramid and the courtyard that compromises the beauty of each. Pei might say that he intended to create this tension. But by what right did he spoil the view of that magnificent space?

The imposition of the pyramid in the courtyard is, I submit, an example of an architect consciously practicing the architecture of the absurd. It is also one of the most powerful examples of how wrong I was in postulating in 1956 that neither architects nor their clients would ever consider commissioning or constructing an absurd building.

26 Pei. Entrance to Louvre, Paris (1989).
Saskia Ltd. © Dr. Ron Wiedencroft.

27 Ludwig Mies van der Rohe. Seagram building, New York, NY (1958).

Hulton Archive/ Getty Images © 2007 Artists Rights Society (ARS), New York.

III

The pervasiveness of these influences inevitably stimulates imitation in architecture as some practitioners strive for the iconic structure that brings instant fame and adulation from architectural critics equally committed to the quest for novelty. I shall narrow my focus to those influences encouraging absurdity internal to the practice of architecture itself, without minimizing the influence of the factors just mentioned.

With the encouragement of historians and critics and on their own, some architects began to think of themselves as fine artists—as artistic geniuses creating habitable large-scale sculptures, landmarks not to be judged in terms of the Beaux-Arts tradition, the Bauhaus principle where form follows and reveals function, the principles of organic architecture, or any other architectural style. These proponents of architecture as sculpture are largely indifferent to the requirements imposed on the architect.

Their dominant influence did not come immediately, for there were architects such as Ludwig Mies van der Rohe who, in his Barcelona Pavilion and his Seagram Building, created in accordance with Bauhaus principles stunning masterpieces in both conception and execution.

He set a standard of architectural purity never surpassed within the International Style. Frank Lloyd Wright, too, gave us definitive

28 Frank Lloyd Wright. Taliesin West, Scottsdale, AZ (begun 1937).
Archivision Inc. © 2007 Frank Lloyd Wright Foundation/Artists Rights Society (ARS), New York.

**29 Wright. Fallingwater,
Bear Run, PA (1935-9).**
Saskia Ltd, © 2007 Dr. Ron
Wiedenhoeft, Frank Lloyd Wright
Foundation/Artists Rights Society
(ARS), New York.

examples of organic architecture in Fallingwater and Taliesin West. It is difficult to imagine structures more fittingly set in their environment. Each is a masterpiece.

It is well known that Wright sketched out the plan of Fallingwater only an hour or so before his client E. J. Kaufmann arrived to inspect his plans. One might have thought Wright would prepare well in advance for this important meeting. Early in his career he was highly respectful of and responsive to the wishes of his clients. No one can imagine an architect more solicitous of a client's wishes than Wright as revealed in his correspondence with Darwin D. Martin while designing his house. Throughout the construction of the Martin residence, Wright sought out his client's opinion and kept Martin informed of his progress.[14]

Wright had his eye on a far greater commission, of course—the Larkin Building, which greatly enhanced Wright's reputation. Martin, a senior executive in the Larkin Soap Company, was influential in the selection of Wright to design the company's headquarters. But after Wright became world famous following the 1923 Tokyo earthquake, which his Imperial Hotel survived while most of the city collapsed, his concern for the needs of his clients dissipated rapidly. The guru took less interest in either his clients' wishes or their pocketbooks. He also often

30 Wright. D.D. Martin residence, Buffalo, NY (1904).

Arts of the United States collection, University of Georgia. © 2007 Frank Lloyd Wright Foundation/Artists Rights Society (ARS), New York.

ignored the science of engineering or the Beaux-Arts expectation that a building should be impervious to rain and free from structural flaws.

E. J. Kaufmann, the department store magnate who commissioned Wright to design Fallingwater, must have been thrilled by the results; still, he must have wished his new house had not fallen so fast. Fearing that Wright's cantilevered balconies were not designed to provide sufficient rigidity, Kaufmann hired his own engineers, who concluded that the balconies required structural reinforcements. When Wright discovered that his specifications had been altered, he insisted, in an all too typical display of arrogance, that the balconies be built according to his original plans. The results were disastrous, as Kaufmann had feared. Shortly after Fallingwater was finished its cantilevers bent, causing its striking balconies to crack and droop. Only major restoration at great expense saved the house for future generations to admire.[15]

Faulty engineering and execution aside, the design of Fallingwater is dramatically fitting. The house seems to spring organically from the hillside of layered rock. Wright's design enhanced the beauty of both the hillside and the house.

Wright's buildings were often strikingly at odds with his verbalizations of them, and his designs were often compromised in their execution.

In 1952 Wright addressed a plenary session of the AIA in the ballroom of the New York Waldorf-Astoria Hotel. I attended with my father. Wright began with a series of rhetorical questions: "Good morning? Good afternoon? Good evening? No way to guess the time of day in this room. Are the acoustics as bad as they appear?" (They were excellent.) Having amused the crowd with his legendary naughtiness, Wright launched into an explanation of his architecture. First, he cautioned, "Young men, never begin your practice in the city in which you plan to live. Make your early, inevitable mistakes out of town." Good advice, as one can see if one looks at Wright's early houses in Mason City, Iowa.

"Gentlemen," he continued, "I declared war on the box, the typical house that imprisons its occupants. I did this by breaking the box at its strongest points, at the corners. My purpose was to liberate the human spirit, to let it soar from within to without, no longer imprisoned by the home. In this I have created a democratic architecture dedicated to human freedom. It is not my fault that this act of liberation should have gone around the world as the cliché of the corner window." And so on in Theoryspeak.

Looking at Wright's early work in Mason City, one can see that Wright was not yet prepared for his "war on the box." Judging by the bizarre emphasis that Wright placed on the solid corners of the Stockman residence, we can only conclude that the box had declared war on Wright—and won decisively in this early engagement.

31 Wright. Stockman Residence, Mason City, IA (1908).
Peter Beers. © 2007 Frank Lloyd Wright Foundation/Artists Rights Society (ARS), New York.

32 Philip Johnson. AT&T building, New York, NY (1978).

33 William Hallett. Chippendale
cabinet (1763).

In the question and answer period, much to the consternation of
my father, I raised my hand and was recognized by the great man. I
said, "In the tradition of English and American common law, a man's
home is his castle. Once you break the close, so that the owner may find
freedom and liberation from the box that has been opened at its corners,
have you not also left the owner at the mercy of the king or tyrant who
can invade his castle through the very same openings through which the
owner could escape?" Wright was not impressed and quickly dismissed
my impertinence.

I greatly admired Wright's prairie houses with their corner windows and broken boxes. I was not commenting on his buildings but on
the absurdity of his explanation. Why, I asked myself, do architects feel
duty-bound to talk aesthetic and philosophic rubbish? And why, more
importantly, are clients impressed and even intimidated by it?

We now know that individuals and institutions will pay for the construction of architectural absurdities. Consider Philip Johnson's AT&T
headquarters and its inspiration.

When Ma Bell willingly pays a distinguished architect and a contractor to construct an office building in the shape of a Chippendale
writing cabinet we are well on our way.

Most absurdist architecture, however, has been built at the bidding of 501(c)3 corporations. CEOs and trustees of museums, symphony orchestras, and especially universities yearn to house their institutions in iconic buildings that Genius has wrought. In such institutions, decisions are made by persons who are not spending their own money, who take no personal financial risk, and who often lack the knowledge and experience in building necessary to ensure that the needs of the institution are met. They are thus often intimidated by smooth-talking, imperious architects and vulnerable to the pretentious jargon that is now the vernacular among both architects and critics. If we wish to understand the strange shapes now imposed on our campuses and cultural centers, we must examine the origins of Genius worship.

IV

No one did more to encourage Genius worship than Sigfried Giedion. Nothing reaches greater heights of pretension and bogus philosophic and historical exposition than his *Space, Time and Architecture*, a work that attributes to Picasso and other Cubists a knowledge of Einstein's special theory of relativity that none possessed. He claimed that artists alone in their "laboratories" work out solutions to aesthetic problems the way scientists carry out explorations of nature. Thus, according to Giedion, art and architecture are not matters on which the public can have a legitimate opinion unless they have been properly trained by artists. The general public has no more legitimate right to comment on art than it does to comment on physics.[16] Art no longer need illumine the human condition or respond to human concerns.

Fortunately, according to Giedion, a small group of artists on the margins—Picasso, Braque, Le Corbusier—decided to carry on "the artist's real work of invention and research." They worked toward "a new conception of space," an aesthetic that baffled the public. Determined to portray the artist as a scientist, Giedion claims—without evidence—that artists followed developments in science and in particular physics. Cubism, Giedion argues, was the attempt of artists to come to grips with non-Euclidean geometry. Cubists, he claims, realized it was no longer possible to present "exhaustive description from one point of reference." "Space in modern physics," he continues, "is conceived of as relative to a moving point of reference, not as the absolute and static entity of the Baroque system of Newton."[17]

Giedion's assumption that artists look to scientists and respond quickly to the latest scientific discoveries is suspect. Non-Euclidean geometries were conceived, we must remember, not at the beginning of the twentieth century, the decade of Cubism's birth, but in the 1820s by Lobachevsky and in the 1850s by Riemann. If it was the conjecture of non-Euclidean geometry that inspired artists, why did it take them eighty years to come up with Cubism? And if it was the publication of Einstein's special theory of 1905 that set them on their hunt, how was it that these artists—abysmally ignorant of advanced tensor mathematics and physics—understood Einstein years before more than a handful of scientists?

More important, Giedion and his admirers ignore the fact that classical architects knew that buildings could be seen simultaneously by different people from many different perspectives, and that each perspective was as valid as any other. We know, for example, that the architects of the Parthenon carefully tapered their columns so that they appeared in balance from a range of perspectives. They also knew, no less than we, that a single person can never view all perspectives simultaneously. Over time, one can see an object from all perspectives and can later remember them. But at any single moment one can see an object from only one perspective.

What, then, is the likely origin of the Cubists' concern in simulating the simultaneous viewing of several perspectives? If artists were influenced by scientific or philosophical ideas it is much more likely that they arrived at the idea of presenting a variety of perspectives in a single work of art from Nietzsche, who in the last decades of the nineteenth century claimed that truth could never be more than perspectival. Nietzsche's philosophy was discussed and well known by artists who created Cubism long before they had any understanding of Einstein's views.

Although Giedion did not recognize Nietzsche's influence on Cubism and, through Cubism, on modern architecture, Nietzsche's influence can be seen in Giedion's own exaltation of architects as Geniuses whose work is beyond the powers of assessment by clients or a reasonably informed public. Architects are now to consider themselves descendants of Nietzsche's Zarathustra, "geniuses" who by right break all laws and conventions. Like Ayn Rand's fictional architect Howard Roark, they behave as if they owe nothing to their clients or the public beyond the gift of their genius. They consider themselves uniquely qualified, insightful, creative wellsprings of ideas, commissioned to stamp the world with their iconic visions.

Some architects needed no prompting by Giedion to assert their rights as Geniuses. Long before the publication of *Space, Time and Architecture*, Le Corbusier inspired Giedion's canonization of architects. Le Corbusier's megalomania was clearly evident in his plans for Algiers.

In 1931 the "Friends of Algiers" invited Le Corbusier to lead two conferences on plans for the city's renewal. By this time he had lost the competition for the League of Nations building in Geneva and had seen the city council of Pessac, France, sabotage a public housing project he had designed. Disgusted with the niceties of democracy, he delved deeper into syndicalism and grew obsessed with Nietzschean themes of bold and direct action. In 1932 he invited the mayor of Algiers to review his grand plans for the city.

Le Corbusier proposed to demolish individual homes and corridor streets and replace the beautiful ancient city with a series of skyscrapers, gigantic apartment complexes on a scale dwarfing those constructed by the Soviets, and an array of elevated highways. In letters to the mayor he insisted that the plans required no more than a "simple decision of the authorities." Le Corbusier continued, "This epoch portends many weighty things. By building, one can orient events towards a solution and future joy."[18]

34 Old Algiers viewed from the Kasbah (1905).

35 "Corridor street" in old Algiers.

The mayor, however, derided Le Corbusier's vision as a mad scheme to "destroy and rebuild completely a city of three hundred thousand residents." He complained that it would "require an absolute dictator controlling not only the goods, but the life of his subjects."[19] Le Corbusier even asked the unelected governor of the French protectorate to overrule the city's elected mayor. "The plan must rule," Le Corbusier wrote. "It is the plan which is right. It proclaims indubitable realities."[20]

When an architect longs to trample over the lives of hundreds of thousands to enact a plan he believes is more real than his fellow men, who must live with his plans while he need not, we can see that it is a short step from "pure architecture" to cruelly absurd, abusive, and debasing dictatorship.

This is not a new or obscure point. Aristotle noted:

There are a number of arts in which the creative artist is not the only, or even the best, judge. These are the arts whose products can be understood and judged even by those who do not possess any skill in the art. A house, for instance, is something which can be understood by others besides the builder: indeed the user of a house—or in other words the householder—will judge it even better than he does.[21]

Or as Samuel Johnson succinctly remarked: "You may scold a carpenter who has made you a bad table, though you cannot make a table."[22]

Le Corbusier's passion for enacting grand schemes over the heads of elected officials led him eventually to head the Vichy government's commission on national building. In 1941 he put his new plans for Algiers at the top of the government's building agenda. Despite Le Corbusier's best efforts, even these Nazi puppets failed to support the towers he envisioned. It would take disciples, aided by trustees and presidents of American universities, to approximate his purposes.

V

One of Le Corbusier's disciples, Josep Lluis Sert, was named dean of the Harvard Design School on the recommendation of Walter Gropius and had a flourishing career as chairman of Harvard's Department of Architecture. His legacy is quite visible in the Boston area. Observing the Holyoke Center shopping mall in the middle of historic Cambridge, and the Peabody Terrace built to house Harvard's graduate students, we

38 Josep Lluis Sert. Holyoke Center, Cambridge, MA (1958).

39 Sert. Peabody Terrace, Cambridge, MA (1962–64).

see the determination of the modern architectural "genius" to defy the tastes and traditions of a community he longs to reshape.

Sert himself denied that he had trampled recklessly on the neighborhoods in which his buildings stood. Describing his work on the Peabody Terrace graduate housing, Sert declared that "it was very important to consider the environment and ties . . . with the city of Cambridge. We could not establish a massive barrier between the neighborhoods behind the site and the riverfront, as many of the older [Harvard] houses had done."[23]

But there is no evidence to support Sert's declaration. Eliot House, one of Harvard's "river houses," faces the Charles River with the Harvard campus, not the local community, behind it.

Sert's Peabody Terrace, by contrast, is superimposed between the residential community and the river. One might ask, which of these structures considers "the environment and ties" with historic Cambridge and New England?

In designing the Peabody Terrace, Sert treated the substantial working-class neighborhood of Cambridge with the same contempt that Le Corbusier showed for Algiers. And for this he was praised. In an article commending Sert's work, Giedion himself hailed Peabody Terrace for fulfilling a "treatment" that "appeared for the first time in Le Corbusier's large unbuilt skyscraper for Algiers, 1931." Giedion even expressed Le Corbusier's same unnerving faith that the plan will triumph

40 Eliot House, Cambridge, MA (1930).

41 Sert. Peabody Terrace.

in the end. Sert's dormitories, Giedion wrote, would become "an integral part of the City of Cambridge *as soon as the slums by which they are partly surrounded have been cleared.*"[24] The Peabody Terrace is not so large as the project Le Corbusier designed for Algiers but, unlike Le Corbusier's project, it was actually built.

Sert's buildings have long worn out their welcome along the Charles River but they still cast a spell over architecture critics fascinated by the siren call of architecture as avant-garde art. Robert Campbell, highly respected architecture critic of the *Boston Globe*, fondly recalls the days he spent as a designer in Sert's studio and celebrates Sert's legacy even as he acknowledges that his work "has lost some of its public acceptance in recent years."[25]

Here we see Peabody Terrace and also the Boston University Law School, one of several buildings Sert designed for Boston University in the decade before I became its president. The next pictures show Boston University's library and the Harvard Science Center, begun two years later.

The kind of repetition seen in these buildings is both lazy and arrogant. Sert seems to have thought he had discovered universal

42 Sert. Peabody Terrace.

43 Sert. Boston University Law School Tower, Boston, MA (1961–66).

"scientific principles" of design to be applied under all circumstances. Hence buildings should look alike without regard to their differences in location and function. Boston University's buildings are distinctive, however, in their flaws.

Thinking perhaps of balmy Spain, Sert designed a large, unprotected entrance to the Mugar Library facing northeast toward the Charles River. The brutal nor'easters of Boston made this entrance unusable.

To avoid flooding the ground floor with rain and snow, the entrance was permanently sealed and a temporary entrance was provided through the adjacent student union. Two decades later, a new protected entrance facing south was added. This excellent addition, designed by the Boston architect William D. Adams, is so thoughtfully and harmoniously conceived that a visitor assumes it is part of Sert's original design. Had Sert used a little common sense and subordinated his genius to the needs of his clients—the students and faculty of the university— he likely would have designed the entrance in a manner similar to the Adams addition.

The Boston University Law School lies on a north/south axis. On a clear winter day the east side is comfortably warmed by the morning sun while the west side suffers from the cold. In the afternoon the situation is reversed.

There is no thermopane, and the narrow colored steel panels for ventilation are hinged and ill-fitting, so that ventilation is plentiful

44 Sert. Boston University Mugar Memorial Library, Boston, MA (1961–66).

45 Sert. Harvard University Science Center, Cambridge, MA (1968–73).

46 Sert. Mugar Memorial Library, former entrance.

47 William Adams. New entrance to Mugar Library, Boston, MA (1983).

48, 49 Sert. Boston University Law School.

whether they be closed or open. Only tiny transom windows can be opened; to wash the windows requires scaffolding and costs in excess of $20,000.

Although it won a prize given by critics devoted to Le Corbusier and his progeny, the Law School, despite its radically different function, is embarrassingly similar to the residential Peabody Terrace visible from our campus. It also leaks and requires constant and expensive maintenance. But it is a gem compared to Boston University's student union as Sert originally designed it.

I suppose again that it was Sert's affection for the benign climate of Spain that prompted him to design the union in Boston around an open patio, surrounded on all sides by high walls.

In summer there was no whiff of a breeze and it was stifling. From October to April, cut off from the sun except from about eleven a.m. to one p.m. with at least a third in umbra at all times due to the southern shift of the winter sun, it served admirably as a pool to trap the rain and snow. Every year the patio, filled with rain or snow, leaked onto the floors below. Continual repairs costing on average $100,000 per year were mandatory.

50 Sert. George Sherman Union, Boston, MA (1961–66).

51 The original patio of George Sherman Union.

I decided to remedy this situation by enclosing the patio. It was difficult to engineer around the limitations Sert had specified in order to prevent any alteration to his plans. But we succeeded, and this wasted, expensive courtyard was transformed by Rothman Partners Architects into a spacious ballroom whose roof sheds water and snow and requires little maintenance.

How could such a mistake have been made in the first place? Sert was engaged by an administration that accepted Giedion's and Le Corbusier's claim that the client knows nothing and that genius must have its way without interference. In a book chapter about Sert's work at Harvard and Boston University, Giedion even praised Sert for "reviving… the house built around a patio." Giedion noted continuity in Sert's work: "The longer he has lived away from Spain… the stronger the Mediterranean note has sounded."[26]

52 The original patio of George Sherman Union in winter.

53 Rothman Partners Architects. Metcalf Ballroom, Boston, MA (1983).

The absurdity of a Spanish patio in the midst of a student union in snowy Boston went unchallenged. It was celebrated. After all, what matters more: where the Genius architect is building or where he was born?

Pretentious exposition had become so common by midcentury that even as fine an architect as Louis Kahn occasionally indulged in high-flown, airy explanations. Kahn, for example, explained to my aesthetics class at Yale why there was no ceiling in his new addition to the Yale Art Gallery.

He explained that honesty and integrity called for the exposure of the overhead structure, with all the duct work and conduits. I asked him why then he had covered all the electrical switches with opaque steel plates. Why not use Plexiglas so that the switch and the wiring would be exposed to ensure integrity and honesty? There was no response, and it

54 Louis Kahn. Yale Art Gallery, New Haven, CT (1951).
Archivision Inc.

55 Kahn. Interior, South Gallery, center vault. Kimbell Art Museum, Fort Worth, TX (1972).
The Kimbell Art Museum, Forth Worth, Texas.

Every time a student walks past a really urgent, expressive piece of architecture that belongs to his college, it can help reassure him that he does have that mind, does have that soul.
—Louis Kahn

YALE UNIVERSITY ART GALLERY

56 Kahn. Yale Art Gallery extension.

didn't matter. The architecture spoke for itself. So why, I asked myself, did Kahn offer "explanations" that led inevitably to inconsistencies? Louis Kahn, who designed the magnificent Kimbell Art Museum in Fort Worth, Texas, had no need to explain, justify, or embellish works that speak volumes for themselves.

The exterior of Kahn's addition to the Yale Art Gallery was a solid wall of beautiful brown brick. I cannot say that it blended well with the older adjacent Beaux-Arts gallery but, like Sert's buildings in relation to Cambridge, its blank wall was a remarkably honest statement of Yale's relations to the people of New Haven—utter exclusion.

However jarring in relation to the original gallery, Kahn's design of the gallery's exterior was at least mercifully free of metaphysics. Unfortunately, long after Kahn's death, someone in authority at Yale pinned to the exterior a huge banner bearing a classic Kahnism. If the exterior of Kahn's building were in fact, as the quotation suggests, a "really urgent expressive piece of architecture," students should have fallen under its spell without Yale's heavy-handed commercial.[27]

Thus far my examples merely adumbrate the recent flood of architectural absurdity. We must now consider a few recent examples of architectural absurdity in full flower by three of our most celebrated architects: Daniel Libeskind, Steven Holl, and Frank Gehry.

Consider Libeskind's Jewish Museum in Berlin. It is based, he says, on a broken Star of David. But where is the star, broken or whole, to be found? The lines of the roof that show the general plan reveal no six-pointed star, fractured or otherwise.

The building zigzags. Having spent hours walking through the building with this question in mind I concluded that Libeskind must have located this broken six-sided star in the three axes found in the basement—the Axis of the Holocaust, the Axis of Emigration, and the Axis of Continuity. Only two of them can be observed at any time and then only in part.

They cross one another in a way similar to runways in a typical small airport where one is laid out north to south, another east to west, and a third crossing each on the diagonal. The three axes—visible simultaneously only on a set of plans but not on the site—give us six end points, which, by some stretch, one can connect in imagination to form a distorted six-pointed star. Alas, it is not actually visible.

Two of these axes end at terminal points. This is appropriate for the Axis of the Holocaust, which ends ominously in a room from which there is no exit. The Axis of Emigration leads to the Garden of Exile with columns from which olive trees are growing. It is built so severely off level that one is disoriented walking about, offering a visceral sense of the insecurity involved in being exiled.

On the other hand, the architect seems to have forgotten that emigration can lead as well to continuity. The present configuration of axes will have an aspect of absurdity until a tunnel is constructed to connect the Garden of Exile to the Axis of Continuity. Otherwise there is no continuity for those exiled. In fact, continuity was found principally in the communities of Jewish exiles gathered in Israel and the United States; together they represent the greatest flowering of German Jewry since 1938.

Form does not follow function in this museum and it has taken genius on the part of the curator to make it work tolerably well despite its appearance and layout. Many interior sections contain exhibits that are

**57 Daniel Libeskind. Jewish
Museum, Berlin, Germany (1999).**
Michael Kappeler/Getty Images.

**58 Libeskind. Jewish Museum.
Interior corridors.**
© 2007 Hartill Art Associates.

powerfully moving, thanks more to the brilliant curator Maren Krüger than to architect Libeskind.

Likewise, one wonders about the purpose behind the cuts on the exterior of the building. These lines, Libeskind explains, suggest locations in Berlin where Jews flourished in the years preceding National Socialism. But I would defy anyone to make sense of them or correlate any of them with specific locations in Berlin. Theoryspeak speaks again.

Anyone who accepts Libeskind's explanation of the slashes on the walls of the Jewish Museum might be surprised to find them making another appearance, this time in his design for an extension to the Royal Ontario Museum in Toronto, Canada.

Upon seeing this repetition, one may wonder: To what locations in Ontario or elsewhere do these cuts refer?

Perhaps aware of this embarrassing repetition of a design gimmick, Libeskind has retreated into Theoryspeak to give this recycled architectural flourish its new purpose. Slashes that in Berlin were supposed to point to the sites of Jewish occupancy are now described as edges of a "crystal, a structure of organically interlocking prismatic forms" that "asserts the primacy of participatory space and public choreography."[28] (Shall we dance?) This bloviation reinforces the suspicion that Libeskind's supposedly somber tribute to the Jews of Berlin was, in truth, just another meaningless architectural absurdity, a trick he justified after the fact with fanciful pronouncements. How many times, one wonders, will Libeskind be able to impress clients and critics with his metaphysical spin-doctoring of senseless contrivances?

If Libeskind had whipped up his confections as sculptures, his visual and verbal nonsense would do little harm. As an architect, however, he has a knack for getting otherwise responsible people and sometimes even entire cities hooked on unrealistic, expensive proposals supported

60 Libeskind. Royal Ontario Museum, Toronto, Canada (2004), rendering of crystal from Bloor Street.
Finest-images, © 2006 The Royal Ontario Museum.

by far-fetched justifications. The most dramatic case of Libeskind over-
dose is the World Trade Center project. In 2002 city and state officials,
along with Larry Silverstein, the holder of the site's lease, unveiled a
design for building again on the site of the towers destroyed in the at-
tacks of September 11, 2001. The proposal, by the firm of Beyer Blinder
Belle, designers of the historical site at Ellis Island, was not exciting but
it had two virtues that would prove salient as the years dragged on. One,
human beings could build it, and two, its modesty would not likely inspire a repeat of September 11.

After an outcry of protest against the blandness of the Beyer
Blinder Belle plans, in part ginned up by the *New York Times*, the Lower
Manhattan Development Corporation decided to scrap the design and
instead hold a public competition for new proposals. In swept Daniel
Libeskind. Libeskind offered New Yorkers an exotic and enticing jumble
of novelties, including a twisting delicate Freedom Tower topped by an
off-center radio transmitter that reached 1,776 feet (get it?); enormous
indoor "Gardens of the World" laced through the building's upper sto-
ries; a wind farm to generate electricity; a cathedral-like atrium filled
with sunlight; and a gap between buildings that, every September 11,
would cast light into the central courtyard for exactly the period between
the first attack (8:46 a.m.) and the collapse of the second tower (10:28
a.m.). Libeskind claimed to have been inspired by rereading the Declaration of Independence, the U.S. Constitution, the poetry of Walt
Whitman, and "The Two Churches," a short story by Herman Melville.[29]

The proposal was utterly Libeskind—basted in portentous but obvious symbolism, festooned with flourishes that suggested fresh, vague
aspirations, and completely impractical. The reed-thin tower that
Libeskind proposed offered little usable floor space in the upper levels; its
twisting shape was dramatic but his design raised doubts about whether
the tower could withstand hurricane winds. It had been easy to sketch
gardens flung a quarter mile into the air but the cost of watering and
heating them appeared to be prohibitive. Most disturbing, Libeskind's
plans did not offer adequate security measures to protect a tower more
enticing to terrorists than the towers it replaced. A truck laden with ex-
plosives could have crashed through the glass walls of the atrium as if
driving through the plastic curtains of a car wash. Libeskind's design
expressed hubris and a penchant for absurdity.

What were the authorities to do? The responsible response would
have been to scrap Libeskind's impractical fantasy immediately and start

61 Beyer Blinder Belle. World Trade Center, New York, NY (2002). Model of site viewed as if from the southwest.
Lower Manhattan Development Corporation.

again. Had the site been under the control of one brave soul, he or she would no doubt have done just that. But during the public competition, New York governor George Pataki, New York City mayor Michael Bloomberg, and Larry Silverstein, the leaseholder, were engaged in a three-way tug-of-war over control of the World Trade Center site. None was going to risk public opprobrium at a time of high-stakes public posturing. Instead they hired Skidmore, Owings and Merrill (SOM), a firm with dozens of skyscrapers to its credit, to try to make the fanciful reaches of Libeskind's design economically and structurally feasible.

SOM tried to fulfill its clients' wishes. In its 2004 design the firm scrapped Libeskind's hanging gardens of Battery Park but kept the delicate glasswork at the top of the Freedom Tower, as well as its gigantic off-center broadcast tower and its twisting, irregular shape.

But even SOM's most experienced architects could not make Libeskind's fantasies practicable, as Silverstein realized during a meeting with engineers in April 2005. "We were looking at each other

and saying, 'My God, this is not going to work with this building,'" Silverstein later told the *New York Times*. "We have to start from scratch."[30] Silverstein had too much of his own money in play and too much experience in construction to be easily intimidated by an eloquent, bullying architect.

In four months of hundred-hour weeks, SOM produced a new design. The parallelogram base from which the tower had twisted up was squared off; the tower itself was straightened into an obelisk of alternating isosceles triangles and given a two-hundred-foot concrete base. When the project was "re-unveiled" in July 2005, critics noted that it bore a striking resemblance to Beyer Blinder Belle's 2002 design.

63 SOM. Freedom Tower, New
York, NY (2006), rendering of
tower and site.

Although serviceable, the latest SOM design has inspired critics to
dismiss it as a fortress, "a symbol of a city still in the grip of fear."[31]
Undeterred, the project's joint developers, Mr. Silverstein and the Port
Authority of New York and New Jersey, began blasting for construction
of the building's foundation in June 2006.

Even with construction of the new Freedom Tower finally under
way, there remained reason to doubt that the project would ever be economically viable. As Nicolai Ouroussoff has noted, in the years since
September 11, 2001, many new projects in other parts of the city, including a twenty-four-million-square-foot development on Tenth Avenue,

have moved forward.[32] With so many options now available, will anyone rent office space in a building that almost surely will be a prime target for terrorists?

In the World Trade Center competition, Libeskind's fanciful design was eventually dismissed by men and women who put practical concerns ahead of the desire to make an extravagant architectural gesture. Libeskind has had better luck, however, intimidating the board members of cultural institutions. Perhaps they lack the business experience and toughness of a man like Silverstein. Perhaps they believe that, however impractical or expensive, cultural centers must make a bold statement that critics will celebrate. Perhaps they lack the courage to question the lofty claims of world-famous architects or the courage to just say no. Whatever the reasons, an uncomfortable truth remains: Libeskind has had far more success winning contracts for museums than for commercial projects.

Libeskind's modus operandi is revealed in the way he won the 1996 competition to design an extension to London's Victoria and Albert Museum. Libeskind proposed to plant a chaotic structure of nonaligned cubes between the wings of the venerable museum. He called the angular structure "the Spiral."[33]

In securing approval of his plans by the board of the Victoria and Albert, Libeskind relied on intimidation. "The board that selected me," Libeskind later told a documentary filmmaker, "are not avant-garde young architects; they're very conservative... When I entered the meeting, it was the names out of Shakespeare—with the Duke of Gloucester presiding." Faced with public distaste for his design, Libeskind skillfully played on both the vanity and the fears of the board's members. He recalled: "I said, 'The V and A is not some dusty institution belonging to local color. It is one of the great world institutions. And it should be competitive in the twenty-first century.'"

Libeskind argued that the board needed to buck up its courage and choose a work of art that would inspire and endure. No work of art, he argued, can be appreciated on its first seeing or hearing. Libeskind claimed that the great works of architecture, like those of music, literature, and art, are understood and appreciated only after several viewings, readings, or hearings. We know, of course, that the works of authors, composers, and artists are, in fact, often heralded on first sight or hearing. The basic problem is that Libeskind asserted the fallacy of the "iconic architects": that a building is fundamentally like a book or

64 Libeskind. Rendering of proposed new wing of Victoria and Albert Museum.
Andrew Putler.

sculpture or piece of music. By means of this conflation the architect is permitted to create like an author, painter, or sculptor without regard for the fact that, unlike books, sculpture, and music, which may be ignored or visited at one's pleasure, a building is lived and worked in and must meet the needs of its users.

Under Libeskind's barrage of intimidation, grounded in the false conflation of architecture and fine art, the V and A Museum's board meekly approved his plan. Libeskind later recalled that "the commissioners actually said, 'You know, we are not a bunch of old fuddy-duddies. We believe that London is not going to be second to any other city. We are going to compete, and architecture is part of a transformation.'" Charles Jencks, architecture critic and Libeskind promoter, was more explicit in describing the role that intimidation had played in Libeskind's success. "Daniel managed to be the needle to prod the Establishment. The British, having been too conservative for too long—too conformist—suddenly got a collective guilty conscience and stuck out their neck and, by a vote of five to four, managed to convince the most conservative part of London—Kensington and Chelsea—to go along with it."[34]

The costs of actually building the Spiral, however, eventually spiraled out of control. Originally budgeted at $72 million, the building's costs had hit $160 million by the spring of 2004. At this point the board of the Heritage Lottery Fund exercised more responsibility than the timid souls at the V and A and effectively killed the project by refusing to donate $27 million to the extension's construction. Despite Libeskind's threat that London would forfeit its international stature if his Spiral were not built, the city has not yet descended into the boondocks. Somehow, even without Libeskind's expensive and impractical building, London remains a world-class city.

Other boards have not had the courage to resist Libeskind's threats. Libeskind's design for the Denver Art Museum is a classic example of

65 Libeskind. Denver Art Museum, Denver, CO (2005).

architecture as sculpture—in this case, a rendering of the carcass of a crashed space shuttle.

Is it appropriate to the client's purpose and his finances? If the client's primary concern is to be the patron of an iconic building, it may be appropriate. But is it the purpose of an art gallery to erect a building that is free-form sculpture of gigantic scale? One can imagine the enormous cost relative to function, and the labyrinthine confusions for visitors to the museum.

Is it consistent with the fiduciary obligations of the museum's trustees to make the museum's home its most expensive sculptural acquisition? Is their endowment such that they can still afford to mount exhibitions and maintain and enlarge their collection? Unless the answers are affirmative the construction would amount to defaulting on their responsibilities in obeisance to proclaimed architectural Genius.

The director and trustees of the Denver Opera House, conscious of their responsibility to reduce costs while meeting the performance needs of the house, selected an architect who bowed to the needs and desires of his client. Peter Lucking of Semple Brown Design melded new construction with the old city hall to create an opera house. No doubt Libeskind would condemn such a modestly conventional building for its lack of daring. David Littlejohn, an arts critic at the *Wall Street Journal*, rightly praised the new opera house for its acoustics, its sight lines for opera and ballet, its amenities and intimacy, and for both its appearance and its practicality. It is, he wrote, "a commodious and ingenious solution to a challenging design problem."[35]

It is an entirely different story when municipal and national governments step in to bail out the projects of less responsible private institutions. When the city of Denver subsidized the Denver Art Museum and the government of Germany helped fund the Jewish Museum in Berlin they became patrons of the architecture of the absurd. The decision makers spent the taxpayers' money, not their own. But in terms of scale and financial resources at their disposal they are relatively conservative patrons compared to Harvard, MIT, and even the much smaller Bard College. Throwing economic considerations to the wind, these institutions have all hired artist/architects to decorate their campuses with paradigms of architectural absurdity.

Consider Harvard's latest venture into graduate housing, One Western Avenue.

66 Machado and Silvetti. One Western Avenue graduate housing, Boston, MA (2003).

One might well question why the architects, both professors at Harvard's Graduate School of Design, chose to build an entirely bland box and then camouflage it with a haphazard range of colors and patterns of brick. If one considers what appears to have been the fate of the dormitory that MIT opened the year before, perhaps this camouflage was intended to protect the building. Harvard may have feared an artillery attack.

Despite its appearance, MIT's Simmons Hall is not meant to resemble dormitories at the universities of Sarajevo or Baghdad. Instead the architect, Steven Holl, says he found inspiration for the design of his building in the sea sponge.

I fail to see the slightest resemblance except that each has lots of holes. The holes of the sea sponge serve a function. The same cannot be said of the holes in Holl's building. Consider the interior.

67 Steven Holl. Simmons Hall,
MIT, Cambridge, MA (2002).

68 Sea sponge.

69 Holl. Simmons Hall, com-
puter lab.

70, 71 Holl. Simmons Hall, "smoke trails" through dorm rooms and hallways.

72 Holl. Simmons Hall.

Note the monotonous series of small windows. They admit light to narrow the pupils of one's eyes while broad, dark mullions widen them. No ophthalmologist would recommend staring into such a wall. Note also the large flues that serve no purpose of ventilation but intrude willy-nilly into corridors, bedrooms, and public rooms.

It is said that they suggest a pattern of rising smoke[36]—marijuana perhaps?

Seen behind a linkage fence, the dormitory takes on somewhat greater coherence if one thinks of a prison. If Frank Lloyd Wright tried in his construction to liberate the human spirit, Holl seems determined to imprison it.

I am not opposed to iconic buildings. If a university, museum, business, or orchestra wishes to create a landmark, and the finances are secure and the building serves its function, I see no reason not to build something bold.

73 Santiago Calatrava. World Trade Center Transit Center, New York, NY, proposal (2004).
Getty Images.

Santiago Calatrava's design for the World Trade Center's new train station, for example, is meant to imitate Gothic cathedrals, which Calatrava has said he likes "for their sincerity, for the way they plainly show their structure."[37] The religious connotation of the Gothic seems particularly appropriate on the site of Ground Zero. For all its flourishes, Calatrava's design is also practical, allowing light to pass from the surface down to platforms below.

This is not merely a matter of form reflecting function but of innovative form allowing for new, appealing functions. Calatrava's practical genius fashions buildings that allow his clients to enjoy them in ways they might not have imagined. Clients may have trouble affording Calatrava designs, which are expensive and time-consuming to build. But when they are finished no one need suffer for his art.

In Los Angeles, Frank Gehry's new concert hall for the Los Angeles Philharmonic has regenerated interest in classical music in a

74 Frank Gehry. Walt Disney Concert Hall, Los Angeles, CA (2003).

city whose rich musical tradition had gone neglected. But there is a difference between Calatrava's work and Gehry's. Calatrava's iconic buildings are both bold and well engineered. The same cannot be said of Gehry's buildings. Neighbors of the new Disney Hall have complained that the hall's shimmering stainless steel curves direct enough sunlight into their apartments to blind them and raise the temperature of their homes by as much as fifteen degrees. Maybe the neighbors are lucky: with a tighter focus the reflecting curves might have set their apartments on fire.[38]

The design of Disney Hall may not be absurd per se, but Gehry's failure to consider the effect of the building on its neighbors is both absurd and inexcusable. Gehry's intrusion of sunlight into neighboring homes is a form of trespass. In the end, the Los Angeles Philharmonic was forced to cover Gehry's bold stainless steel shapes with a matte-finished cloth, adding to the building's cost and replacing the glamour of the original material with a cheap-looking cover. It reminds one of an evening gown made of burlap.

Many of Gehry's iconic buildings do not even have the benefit of excellent form. Bard College has a lovely campus in New York's Hudson Valley and it is known for its outstanding programs in music. Its president, Leon Botstein, a distinguished musician and conductor, has built a fine orchestra. Recently he hired (or turned the college's affairs and fortune over to) Frank Gehry to construct a performing arts center.

It is hard to discern what Gehry hoped to accomplish with this design. On the one hand, the building resembles somewhat an overgrown peasant's cottage, with stainless steel replacing the traditional thatch. Or perhaps the building was constructed from scraps of computer-generated metal sections left over from Bilbao. Here again is architecture as sculpture, suggesting, perhaps unfairly, the sculpture of Henry Moore.

However, move to the side and the back (not simultaneously, of course, but as rapidly as is humanly possible). Now we see the ungainly

76 Gehry. Richard B. Fisher Center for the Performing Arts, Bard College, Annandale-on-Hudson, NY (2003).

absurd forms and the utter incongruity of the design. Evidently there were not enough scraps left over from Bilbao.

The huge overhangs never fit together but overlap and cross and are shockingly large for no obvious purpose unless to prostrate all visitors before the gigantic ego of the architect. But the relation of the computer-designed and undulating steel forms to the prosaic boxy rear of the center reminds me, and perhaps others, of the movie set in *Blazing Saddles*—all facade and nothing worth seeing behind.

If the undulating metal forms have become the trademark of Gehry's buildings, so, unfortunately, have their skyrocketing costs. In 1997 the city of Chicago decided to extend Grant Park by refurbishing twenty-four acres of abandoned railroad tracks on its northern side. Gehry was hired to design the park's centerpiece and overall plan. He won the commission, in part, by estimating that the park would cost $150 million and promising to complete it in time to host celebrations of the new millennium. In fact, however, the park's main buildings were

82 Gehry. Pritzker Pavilion, Chicago, IL (2004).

Howard Ash Photography.

83 Gehry. IAC Headquarters, New York, NY (2006).

Albert Vecerka/Estostock.

finished four years late and cost $475 million, an overrun of $325 million, or more than 200 percent.[39]

Gehry's main contribution to the park was the outdoor amphitheater itself, the Jay Pritzker Pavilion, named for the man who founded America's most prestigious architecture prize. With four thousand fixed seats and space for another seven thousand people on the lawn, the Pritzker Pavilion is a major addition to Chicago's performance space.

Despite the high price, Chicago got very little that was distinct. The pavilion features a mammoth proscenium reminiscent of the entrance to Bard's Fisher Hall, as well as the wispy metal sheets and awkwardly exposed superstructure that characterizes Gehry's work for Los Angeles, Bard College, and Bilbao.

Gehry's latest project, the Manhattan headquarters of Barry Diller's internet empire, is more restrained than his other recent work. The translucent walls of the IAC headquarters are elegantly smooth. The curving facade does not splay apart into shards that jut out at random angles. Instead, the building's lines bend evenly down to the ground like sails to a deck.

Some architecture critics wonder if Gehry is growing tame. "These easy, fluid forms are a marked departure from the complex, fragmented structures of his youth," the *New York Times'*s Nicolai Ouroussoff

wrote. "Rather than mining rich new creative territory, Mr. Gehry, now 78, seems to be holding back."[40]

I doubt that the restraint apparent in this building can be attributed to Gehry. I suspect rather that it is the restraint of an intelligent and determined client sophisticated in economic issues. Barry Diller is a major entrepreneur used to taking risks—but not foolish ones. As a former Hollywood executive Diller surely knows the dangers of being dragged into a financial morass by undisciplined and self-indulgent talent; as CEO of a company in need of a functioning building he had a strong incentive to review Mr. Gehry's designs, expenses, and timetables. Gehry would have found it difficult to convince Diller of the aesthetic importance and economic value of his typically disjointed buildings. But most important, I believe that Mr. Diller was watchful because, unlike the trustees of Bard College and the Los Angeles Philharmonic and the city officials in Chicago, he was spending his own money.

I am not critical of Gehry's twisted metal shapes because they are different but because too often they make no sense, are out of scale, wastefully expensive, and on the underside offer not the honest exposure of Louis Kahn but what seems more akin to indecent exposure.

The documentary film *Sketches of Frank Gehry*, a sympathetic portrait directed by Gehry's friend Sydney Pollack, revealed the problem: Gehry thinks of himself not so much as an architect but an artist, a sculptor or a painter. Recalling his early years in Los Angeles, Gehry explained why he preferred the company of artists. "My colleagues who were doing architecture . . . were making fun of what I was doing. . . . And here were these funny artists—I just loved their work—who were treating me as part of the team." The problem with architecture, Gehry complains, is that "there are sort of rules about architectural expressions; they have to fit into a certain channel. Screw that. Doesn't mean anything. I'm going to do what I do best, and if it's no good, the marketplace will deny it."[41]

Unfortunately the marketplace is not known for its elevated taste; it has placed its seal of approval on trash as often as on quality. As *Sketches of Frank Gehry* reveals, Gehry has no need to fear the market; he has used his remarkable persuasive powers to convince clients to build his large-scale sculptures. Hollywood agent Michael Ovitz happily calls Gehry "a contemporary Cubist and sculptor." This lapidary statement nonetheless indicates the profound deficiency in many of Gehry's works. His misconception, like that of Libeskind, that architecture has

84 Joern Utzon. Sydney Opera House, Sydney, Australia (1956–73).

no distinct purpose or consequent limitations that distinguish it fundamentally from painting and sculpture has led him to impose on clients works that are profligate in cost and grotesquely unaccommodating to their purpose. Perhaps there will always be clients who are happy to fulfill Gehry's artistic ambitions, despite the waste and inutility inevitable when architecture is practiced as a fine rather than as a practical art. But great architecture does not depend on, rather is compromised by, this confusion. Many superb architects—who know that the limitations of architecture are to be respected rather than "screwed"—create splendid buildings while fulfilling the goals of their clients.

I greatly admire the unusual shapes in the work of the Danish architect Joern Utzon, who designed the Opera House in Sydney, Australia. It is located on a point of land surrounded by water, and from a distance it floats as a lovely sailing ship. But it also works well as a group of concert halls, even though it was not completed as Utzon intended.

In 1966 Utzon resigned from overseeing construction of the Opera House after an election gave Australia a new minister of public works unsympathetic to the project. Utzon's replacement, Peter Hall, cut corners by altering the building's two major venues; he also moved the theater for drama into the podium of the building. The fundamentals of Utzon's design were so sound that the Opera House has nevertheless been a hugely successful venue for opera and concerts. Two members of Boston University's faculty, Anthony di Bonaventura and Phyllis Curtin, performed there and reported that the acoustics were outstanding. Only the theater, a space Utzon did not design, has proved inadequate.

The Opera House's performance halls are now being thoroughly renovated to restore the architect's original design. The clumsy wood paneling that Hall had affixed directly to the concrete shell is being replaced by carefully shaped plywood ceilings that will be suspended from the shell and further enhance the acoustics. As the Sydney architect Richard Johnson observed, "The auditorium is the musical instrument; the shell is the case."[42]

The Sydney Opera House is an iconic structure that, despite alterations from the architect's original intent, merits all the praise that has been heaped upon it. Like the creations of Gaudí it is imaginative and excitingly and enduringly novel. If completed according to Utzon's intentions it should, like Gaudí's creations, be coherent, beautiful, and functional.

There are many contemporary architects who bring curvilinear and rectilinear lines into an innovative harmony. One thinks of the work of Fay Jones and Moshe Safdie.

In Cambridge, the firm of Stubbins Associates has transformed, on time and under budget, a local landmark, a former factory of the New England Confectionery Company, into a research center for Novartis, a Swiss pharmaceutical firm. Stubbins Associates preserved the elegant rectilinear windows and doors of the building's facade. Inside, by contrast, the central core of stairs and elevators is curvilinear, reflecting the undulating pattern of the giant strand of DNA embedded in the French granite of the central lobby floor. Above it, undulating balconies overlooking the central atrium cut through the building's core.

The renovation reflects the continuity and change in its purpose. The building is still a factory but it is now engaged in the discovery and production of new drugs developed from the human genetic code.

The buildings of Jones, Safdie, and Stubbins Associates are every bit as contemporary as those of Gehry, Holl, and Libeskind, but the for-

85 Fay Jones. Mildred B. Cooper Memorial Chapel, Bella Vista, AK (1988).
Timothy Hursley/The Arkansas Office.

86 Moshe Safdie. Yitzhak Rabin Center, Tel Aviv, Israel (2002), accepted proposal.

87 Safdie. Yitzhark Rabin Center under construction.

**88 Stubbins Associates.
Novartis Center, Cambridge,
MA (2004).**

**89 Stubbins Associates.
Novartis Center.**

mer have been designed to give their clients beautiful buildings that are not excessive in either design or cost and that are well suited to their functions. They were designed by brilliant architects who know their art, their craft, and their business: architects who consider beauty, utility, and economy more important than shock and waste.

Now to the pièce de résistance of absurdity in architecture: the Stata Center at MIT.

William J. Mitchell, dean of MIT's School of Architecture at the time Gehry was hired, claimed that the building would unite divided scientists, researchers, and students who were once housed in MIT's Building 20, where radar was developed. Yet it is difficult to see how scientists, researchers, and students could be divided in a structure so obviously unified as Building 20. (Even today those scientists who worked in Building 20 praise its simplicity, flexibility, and the way it supported their research.)[43] It is even more difficult to imagine how the occupants of the Stata Center can possibly be united in a building as fractured as Gehry's creation.

Dean Mitchell reported that the building would have 430,000 square feet of space. It was supposed to cost about $100 million,[44] or about $232 per square foot. With cost overruns, however, the price is now estimated at $315 million, more than three times the original estimate. MIT claims that the $100 million did not budget for an underground garage later added to the design. The new design, including the garage and totaling 713,000 gross square feet, was supposed to cost $165 million, or $231 per square foot. By coming in at $315 million instead, the Stata Center cost $442 per square foot, nearly twice the revised budget. Even if we accept the square foot costs of the garage as equal to the square foot cost of the building itself, it does not explain or justify the huge cost overrun in the final construction. In addition, the building was completed four years past the expected date, and to the extent that time is money the cost overrun was substantially increased.

This is vintage Gehry, whose contempt for the interests of clients and whose narrow dedication to his sculptural conception leave him indifferent to sordid issues of cost and time. When Gehry is hired, the partnership of client and architect is virtual except when it comes to paying the bill.

Some have defended MIT's decision to build expensive, flashy buildings as a way to prime the fund-raising pump. As one Boston consultant recently told the *Boston Globe*: "If you have an exciting building, a Stata Center, for example, you're in a position to say to a prospective donor, 'You can have your name on this.' People like to be associated with fresh and exciting things, and architecture can be one of them."[45] But naming gifts are rarely more than a fraction of the estimated cost of a building, a minuscule fraction when there is a massive cost overrun. And there are donors who disdain contributing to an institution willing to waste monies on expensive, defective architectural monstrosities.

90 Gehry. Stata Center, MIT, Cambridge, MA (2004).

Sometimes, moreover, the well runs dry. In 1990 the board of the American Center in Paris agreed to sell their headquarters and hire Gehry to design a new facility for them. The board bet that a new, high-profile building would reinvigorate the center and attract new donations to support an institution that had introduced French audiences to American culture for nearly six decades. In this case Gehry accurately estimated the cost of constructing his design at $41 million. But this left only $1 million to spare from the $42 million received from the sale of the old facility. The center managed to keep Gehry's building open for nineteen months. But with no significant increase in philanthropy, the center had no way to meet its annual operating costs of $6 million. The center, once a home away from home in Paris for American artists, was forced to shut its doors in 1996.[46] The folly of accepting Gehry's extravagant proposal lay with the board of the American Center. They let vain ambition to own an iconic building blind them to obvious economic realities. With eyes open, they spent themselves out of business.[47]

MIT is financially strong, but the Stata Center has exacted a heavy toll. The institute froze salaries in 2003–2004 and announced plans to trim 250 jobs the following year. Undoubtedly MIT's cost cutting was inspired by factors other than the expense of any one building, but an overrun of $215 million didn't help.

To appreciate how little function MIT has bought for its $315 million, one must step inside the Stata Center.

Gehry had an agenda in designing the Stata Center: he wanted to force the center's brilliant scientists to interact. He had two strategies.

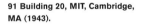

91 Building 20, MIT, Cambridge, MA (1943).

92, 93 Gehry. Stata Center, interior details.

First, he would break down the walls of their offices, leaving them open in order for colleagues to stop by. Second, he would drive a pedestrian "street" through the heart of the building, endowing the center with the feel of a friendly neighborhood.

Gehry, ignorant of or indifferent to the needs and methods of researchers, wanted the center's scientists to work without walls. But his arrogance was opposed by professors who insisted that he close off their spaces with glass. "It's like orangutans," Gehry told the *Financial Times*. "They retreat to the tree-tops for privacy and come down when they want to be sociable."[48]

The outlines of the open jungle gym Gehry had wanted to build, now enclosed by glass, are still clearly visible. The glass may reduce some of the building's noise, but the visual distractions of foot traffic outside are hardly conducive to sustained concentration. Nor, of course, do glass walls offer adequate privacy. In this sense, Gehry's design has given the Stata Center the worst aspects of small town life. Talk to a

94, 95 Gehry. Stata Center, interior details.

colleague about a work issue or personal problem and the whole "town" knows with whom you are speaking.

If snooping is part of life in a small town, at least the stakes are pretty minor. Not so at the Stata Center, where important secret military and industrial research is carried out. The center is home, for example, to MIT's Cryptography and Information Sharing Group, charged with designing the "practical engineering of secure information systems." Thanks to the design of their building, they may inadvertently share more information than they secure.

The "street" that Gehry envisioned for the ground floor of the Stata Center might have been a success. Connecting a gym, a child care facility, and a food court, the central corridor might have been a genuinely friendly gathering place. Unfortunately, Gehry's pretentious ambitions got in the way. Just look at the huge blackboards and walls of cork Gehry tossed in as sites for "spontaneous" creation.

96, 97 Gehry. Stata Center, interior "street."

96, 97 Gehry. Stata Center, interior "street."

98 Gehry. Stata Center, interior "street."

99 Gehry. Stata Center, interior, with wall photographs.

100 Gehry. Stata Center, skylights near faculty dining hall.

The emptiness of the corridor shows that Gehry, while pontificating on the living habits of faculty and students, does not in fact understand how they actually like to work. Maybe they gossip or even discuss ideas in general while waiting in line for a kebab. But when it comes to thinking, planning, and drawing up designs, they prefer the privacy of their offices. The corridor's blackboards are of no use for serious scientists, even if they delight children and graffiti artists.

The building's ambitions have also run ahead of its overextended budget. On the central corridor one was supposed to find interactive multimedia displays of work going on in the building. But cost overruns have left the wooden frames meant for terminals and televisions to be covered with enormous photographs printed on canvas. Gehry has managed to turn the architect's trade on its head. Better architects make cheap materials look expensive. Gehry has spent a fortune on a building whose interior, covered with canvas and furnished with plywood, looks cut-rate. Gehry's work brings to mind a comment attributed to Dolly Parton about her appearance: "It takes a whole lot of money to look this cheap."

Finally, there is the classic problem plaguing all too many Gehry buildings, and all buildings built as absurdist sculpture rather than as functioning facilities. Can they keep out the rain? The Stata Center's flat glass roofs and innumerable joints subject to expansion and contraction guarantee leakage from winter snow and summer rain. Like forensic scientists investigating a crime scene, MIT professors patiently mark and number each new leak.

Undeterred, Dean Mitchell is pleased with the center and says: "Stata is [Gehry's] . . . most complex program and intellectual agenda. I think it *may* be the best thing he's done."[49] Think on that!

102 Tomie dePaola's
Mother Goose.

I have a simpler, more down-to-earth assessment. Again, consider the building. It reminds me of something from Mother Goose, which I learned at my mother's knee. Perhaps you remember the verse:

> **There was a crooked man**
>
> **And he walked a crooked mile,**
>
> **He found a crooked sixpence**
>
> **Against a crooked stile;**
>
> **He bought a crooked cat**
>
> **Which caught a crooked mouse,**
>
> **And they all lived together**
>
> **In a little crooked house.**[50]

Architecture of the absurd is flourishing thanks to the debasement, inexperience and supine gullibility of the clients. What is the cure? Perhaps re-reading Hans Christian Andersen's insightful fairy tale "The Emperor's New Clothes" will help. The client—not the architect—is the emperor; it is he who is mocked when architects forget their function as practical artists in partnership with clients whose views are worthy of respect and whose economic resources are not to be exceeded. The patrons, the clients —the ones who pay—should not forfeit their dignity as persons and allow themselves, through vanity, gullibility, or timidity, to be seduced. Clients should not be flummoxed by architects who overstep the practical limitations of their profession. Theoryspeak, celebrity, and self-proclaimed Genius cannot cover the naked absurdity of much contemporary architecture.

Notes

1. We are indebted to Alexander Caragonne for rescuing from obscurity this important moment in the history of architecture. His book *The Texas Rangers: Notes from an Architectural Underground*, published in 1995 by the MIT Press, gives a remarkably detailed account.

2. Quoted in Donald Weismann, *The 12 Cadavers of Joe Mariner: With Screenplay by the Author and Lee Marvin*, second edition (Express Press, 2002), from the prologue.

3. Weismann, *The 12 Cadavers of Joe Mariner* (Austin: Pemberton Press, 1977). The first edition did not include the screenplay version of the story.

4. Von Hagens's "works" are now showing in several venues under the title "Body Worlds." Premier Exhibitions' "Bodies . . . The Exhibition" has shown in Atlanta, Tampa, and New York. I would not discuss "Bodies . . . The Exhibition" in the same breath with von Hagens's exhibition did they not share a lack of respect for the sanctity of human remains. Neither exhibit offers adequate proof that the bodies are on display with the permission of the deceased's next of kin. Bodies for both exhibits were supplied by Dalain University in northern China, where officials have been implicated in providing, without authorization of the next of kin, the bodies of executed prisoners. This has been reported credibly by the Chinese human rights activist Harry Wu and the *New York Times*. (See *New York Times*, August 20, 2005, p. A15 ff, and *New York Times*, November 18, 2005, p. A24.)

It must be acknowledged, however, that "Bodies . . . The Exhibition" attempts to disavow the artistic pretensions of von Hagens's show. "Bodies" does display some corpses in poses that reveal an artistic conceit; it features, for example, a skinless, partially dissected body positioned as Rodin's *Thinker* and others posed as orchestra conductors, violinists, and athletes. For the most part, however, the exhibition is presented as a scientific study of human anatomy. Viewing this exhibit is like looking over the shoulder of Vesalius as he dissected human corpses. The sight of lungs destroyed by emphysema ought to convince anyone to give up smoking and the series of ten– to fourteen–week old fetuses on display reminds us how quickly our unborn young take human form.

5. Herbert Muschamp, "A Building's Bold Spirit, Clad in Marble and Controversy," *New York Times*, November 24, 2003, p. E1.

6. John Rockwell, "Shocking! Offensive! But Being Pleasant Is Beside the Point," *New York Times*, November 14, 2003, p. E1.

7. See "Edward Albee, Still Playing Rough," *Boston Globe*, March 7, 2004, p. N4.

8. Personal correspondence, Tom Wolfe to John Silber, December 2, 2003.

9. Attributed to Andy Warhol, 1967.

10. Robert Smithson, interviewed by Kenneth Baker, in Lynne Cooke and Karen Kelly, eds., *Robert Smithson Spiral Jetty: True Fictions, False Realities* (Berkeley: Dia Foundation/University of California Press, 2005), pp. 157–58.

11. Robert Smithson, "Cultural Confinement," in Jack Flam, ed., *Robert Smithson: Collected Writings* (Berkeley: University of California Press, 1996), p. 157.

12. The Whitney's description is at http://whitney.org/exhibition/feat_smithson.html.

13. The company changed its name in 2000 to John Hancock Financial Services.

14. See Jack Quinan, *Frank Lloyd Wright's Martin House* (Princeton, N.J.: Princeton Architectural Press, 2004), especially chapter 4.

15. See Ada Louise Huxtable, *Frank Lloyd Wright* (New York: Lipper/Viking, 2004).

16. See Sigfried Giedion, *Space, Time and Architecture* (Cambridge: Harvard University Press, 1941), p. 430 ff.

17. Ibid., p. 429.

18. Letter from Le Corbusier to M. Brunel, mayor of Algiers, December 10, 1932. Reproduced in Mary McLeod, "Le Corbusier and Algiers," *Oppositions* 19/20 (Winter/Spring 1980), p. 82.

19. Letter from M. Brunel, mayor of Algiers, to Le Corbusier, December 26, 1932. Reproduced in ibid., p. 82–83.

20. Quoted in ibid., p. 70.

21. Ernest Barker (trans.), *The Politics of Aristotle* (Oxford: Oxford University Press, 1946), p. 126.

22. James Boswell, *Boswell's Life of Johnson*, vol. 1 (Oxford: Clarendon Press, 1934–64), p. 409.

23. Quoted in Robert Campbell, "Harvard Exhibitions Showcase Sert as the Soul of Collaboration," *Boston Globe*, October 13, 2003, p. N2.

24. Sigfried Giedion, "New Ventures in University Building," *Zodiac* 16 (1966), p. 24–35.

25. Campbell, "Harvard Exhibitions Showcase Sert Collaboration."

26. Sigfried Giedion, *S. José Luis Sert; architecture, city planning, urban design* (New York: Praeger, 1967), p. 7. (Sert referred to himself by his Catalan name, Josep Lluis Sert.)

27. Although the quotation is Kahn's, it was the decision of some nameless barbarian to affix it to his building.

28. Daniel Libeskind, "Renaissance ROM," at http://www.daniel-libeskind.com/projects/pro.html?ID=45.

29. Paul Goldberger, "Urban Warriors," *The New Yorker*, September 15, 2003, p. 74.

30. Glenn Collins, "For the Design Team, a Desperate Rush," *New York Times*, July 10, 2005, p. 25.

31. Nicolai Ouroussoff, "A Deepening Gloom about Ground Zero's Future," *New York Times*, September 10, 2005, p. 9.

32. Ibid.

33. One wonders why Libeskind called this angular structure a "spiral." Was he attempting an angular version of the internal spiral of Wright's Guggenheim Museum?

34. All quotations are taken from *Daniel Libeskind*, R.A.M. documentary for V.P.R.O., directed by Rob Schroeder, the Netherlands, 2004.

35. David Littlejohn, "New Music, New Opera House in Denver," *Wall Street Journal*, September 22, 2005, p. D8.

36. Robert Campbell, "MIT's New Dorm Is Extraordinary, Inside and Out," *Boston Globe*, October 20, 2002, p. N4.

37. "Innovators Forging the Future," *Time*, March 8, 2004.

38. "Glare from Disney Hall Heating Up Condos," The Associated Press, Feb. 24, 2004. Disney Hall is not the first Gehry building to blind its neighbors. The Frederick R. Weisman Art Museum, the teaching museum of the University of Minnesota, also has a skin of highly-reflective polished metal. The Museum is located on the western bank of the Mississippi River and at one end of Minneapolis' heavily-traveled Washington Avenue Bridge. In the afternoon, sun reflecting off the Museum's western panels blinds drivers on this busy thoroughfare.

39. "Late, Sure, but Chicago Thinks Big," *Chicago Sun-Times*, July 16, 2004, p. 46.

40. Nicolai Ouroussoff, "Gehry's New York Debut: Subdued Tower of Light." *The New York Times*, March 22, 2007.

41. All quotations are from *Sketches of Frank Gehry*, directed by Sydney Pollack (Sony/WNET, 2006).

42. Geraldine Brooks, "Unfinished Business," *The New Yorker*, October 17, 2005, p. 102.

43. As reported to me by one of the scientists who worked in Building 20.

44. As reported by *The Tech*, September 19, 2003. See: http://www.tech.mit.edu/V123/N41/41StataGlobe2.41n.html.

45. Catherine Donaher, quoted in "Starchitecture on Campus," *Boston Globe Magazine*, February 22, 2004.

46. "American Center in Paris Must Sell Its Home," *New York Times*, January 24, 1996, p. C15.

47. After closing the American Center the center's board fired its staff and tried for two years to sell the Gehry building. In 1998 the French government paid $21 million for it, far less than one half of its original cost in constant dollars. The French then spent $40 million and seven years to remodel the building for use by the Cinémathèque Française. After ending operations for several years the center is back, but on a very limited basis. See "A New Life for a Has-Been, a Gehry Building," *New York Times*, October 26, 2005, p. B1.

48. "The Perils of Designing for MIT's Geniuses," *Financial Times*, May 28, 2004.

49. Quoted in "Questions Build Right Along with MIT's Stata Center," *Boston Globe*, September 11, 2003, p. D1.

50. Rhyme and image from Tomie dePaola's *Mother Goose* (Toronto: General Publishing, 1985), p. 24.

Additional Photo Credits and Permissions

Image number:

1. Allan Kohl.

7. Courtesy cottinglyconnect.org.uk.

8. Editorial Escudo de Oro, S.A.

9. Philipp Holzmann/Structurae Image Licensing.

10. Renaud Visage Photography.

13. Jacques Mossot/Structurae Image Licensing.

15. Nicolas Janberg/Structurae Image Licensing.

16. Archives of Antonio Gaudí.

17, 18. Patricia E. Arriaza.

19. Brochure for "Prof. Gunther von Hagens' Körperwelten: Die Faszination des Echten," Halle, 1999.

22. Buddy Mays/Travel Stock Photography.

24. Naomi Miller.

25, 38, 39, 40, 41, 42, 43, 45, 47, 48, 49, 56, 66, 67, 69, 70, 71, 72, 74, 75, 77, 78, 79, 80, 81, 90, 92, 93, 94, 95, 96, 97, 98, 99, 100, 101. Chandler Rosenberger.

32. Oliver Radford/Boston University Department of Art History.

33. J.A. Lewis and Son.

34. Fryer Library, University of Queensland Library, UQFL10, Image #646.

35. Carfree.com.

44, 46, 50, 51, 52, 53. Boston University Photo Services.

59. Thomas Mueller/Photographers Direct.

63. Courtesy Silverstein Properties.

65. John N. Pozadzides.

76. Rachel E. Hyman.

84. Michele Falzone.

86, 87. Courtesy Moshe Safdie.

88, 89. Courtesy Novartis Institutes for Biomedical Research.

91. Building 20 Photographic Documentation Project Records, Institute Archives and Special Collections, MIT Libraries.

102. Tomie dePaola, from *Tomie dePaola's Mother Goose* © 1985 Tomie dePaola, illustrations. Used by permission of G.P. Putnam's Sons, A Division of Penguin Young Readers Group, A Member of Penguin Group (USA) Inc, 345 Hudson Street, New York, NY 10014. All rights reserved.

Index

Page numbers in *italics* refer to illustrations.